Taormina
Italy

City Map

 Glob:us

Taormina, Italy — City Map
By Jason Patrick Bates

First Edition: February 2017

Scale ⁄ 1:4000

▮▮▮▮▮▮ 50m

▮▮▮▮▮▮▮▮▮▮▮▮▮ 500ft

Map Overview

Map Symbols

▬	Highway		Map continuation page
▬	Street	····	Path
	Archaeological site		Kiosk
	Artwork	✕	Level crossing
	Atm		Library
	Bar		Lighthouse
	Bicycle rental		Memorial
	Biergarten		Memorial plaque
	Buddhist temple		Monument
	Bus station		Museum
	Bus stop		Muslim mosque
	Cafe		Neighbourhood
	Camping site		Nightclub
	Car rental		Parking
	Cave entrance	▲	Peak
	Chalet		Pharmacy
	Charging station		Picnic site
†	Church / Monastery		Playground
	Cinema		Police
	Courthouse		Post office
	Department store		Prison
	Dog park		Pub
	Drinking water		Railway
	Dry cleaning		Restaurant
	Elevator		Shinto temple
	Embassy		Sikh temple
	Fast food		Sports centre
⚓	Ferry terminal		Supermarket
	Fire station		Taoist temple
	Fountain		Taxi
	Fuel		Telephone
	Golf course		Theatre
	Guest house		Toilets
	Hindu temple		Townhall
	Hospital		Traffic signals
	Hostel		Viewpoint
	Hotel		Water park
i	Information		Wilderness hut
	Jewish synagogue		Windmill

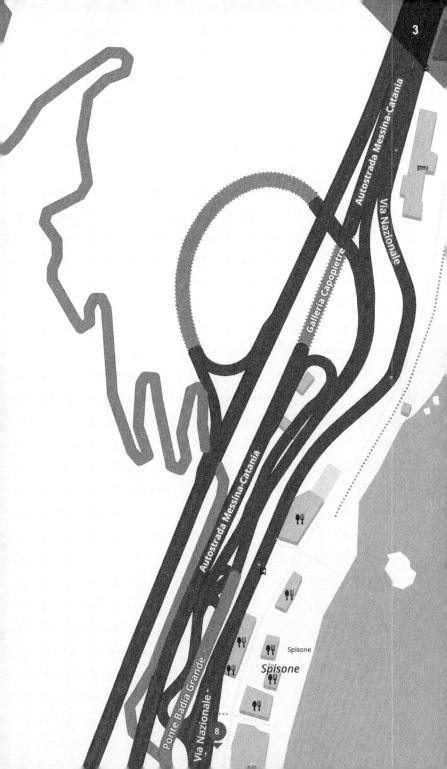

Autostrada Messina-Catania

Via Nazionale

Galleria Capopietre

Autostrada Messina-Catania

Spisone

Spisone

Ponte Badia Grande

Via Nazionale

8

Scalazza

Via

Via

Salita delle Ginestre

Piazza Cacciola

Via Fontana Vecchia

Via dietro

13

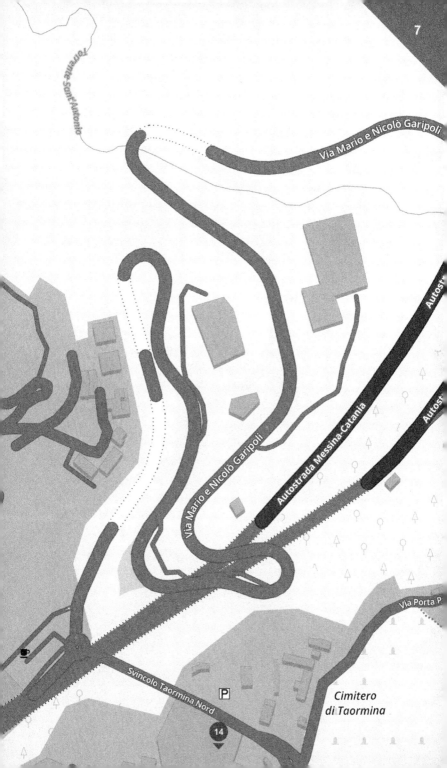

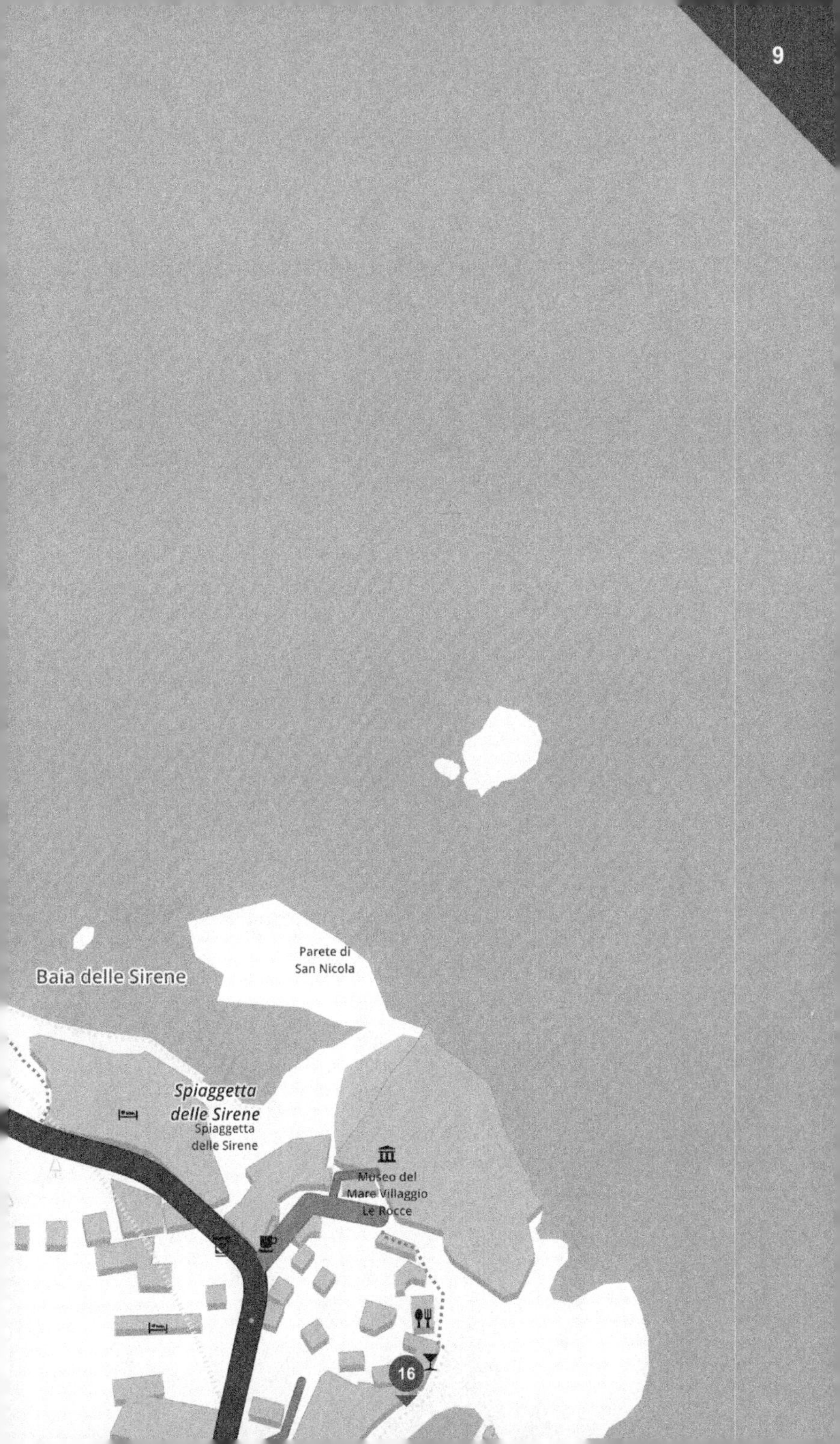

Parete di
San Nicola

Baia delle Sirene

Spiaggetta
delle Sirene
Spiaggetta
delle Sirene

🏛
Museo del
Mare Villaggio
Le Rocce

16

4

Via Rober

Viadotto Sirina

19

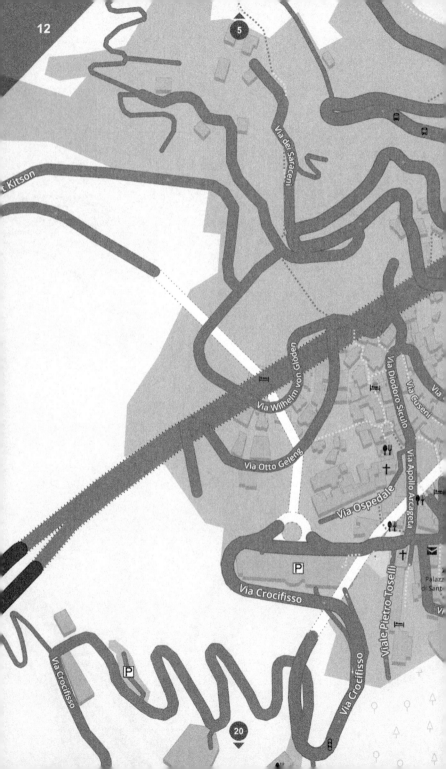

Kitson

Via dei Saraceni

Via Wilhelm von Gloeden

Via Otto Geleng

Via Diodoro Siculo

Via Guseni

Via

Via Apollo Arageta

Via Ospedale

Via Crocifisso

Viale Pietro Toselli

Via Crocifisso

Via Crocifisso

Palazz
di Sant

Vi

5

20

P

P

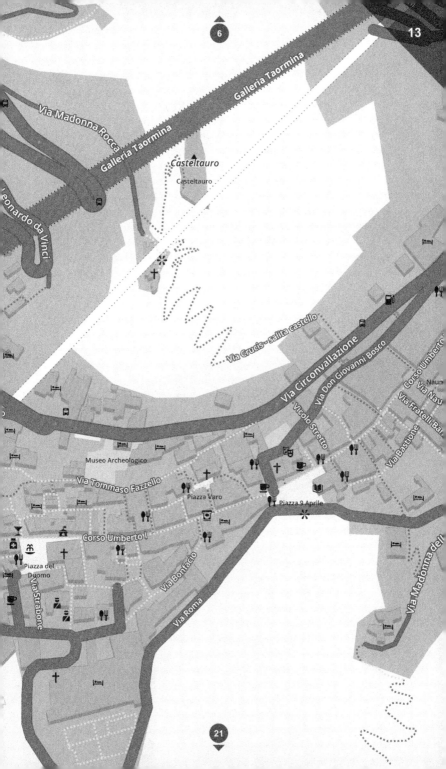

Via Madonna Rocca

Galleria Taormina

Galleria Taormina

Galleria Taormina

Leonardo da Vinci

Casteltauro

Casteltauro

Via Crucis – salita castello

Via Circonvallazione

Via Don Giovanni Bosco

Corso Umberto

Naun

Via Nau

Vicolo Stretto

Via Fratelli Bat

Via Bastione

Museo Archeologico

Via Tommaso Fazzello

Piazza Varo

Piazza 9 Aprile

Corso Umberto I

Piazza del Duomo

Via Strabone

Via Bonfacio

Via Roma

Via Madonna del

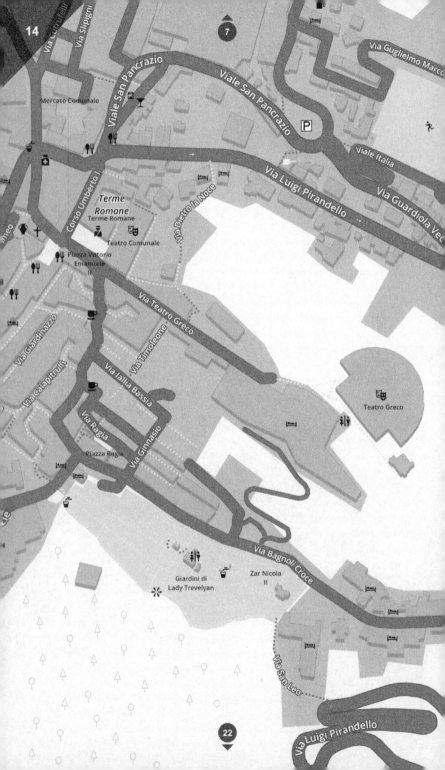

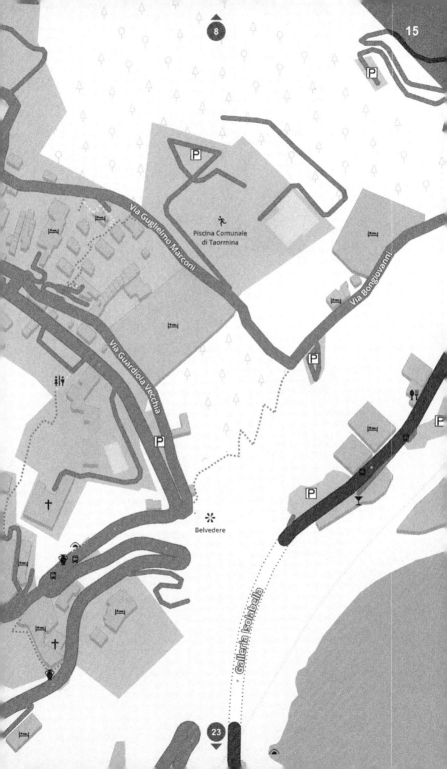

8

Via Guglielmo Marconi

Piscina Comunale
di Taormina

Via Bongiovanni

Via Guardiola Vecchia

Belvedere

Galleria Isolabella

23

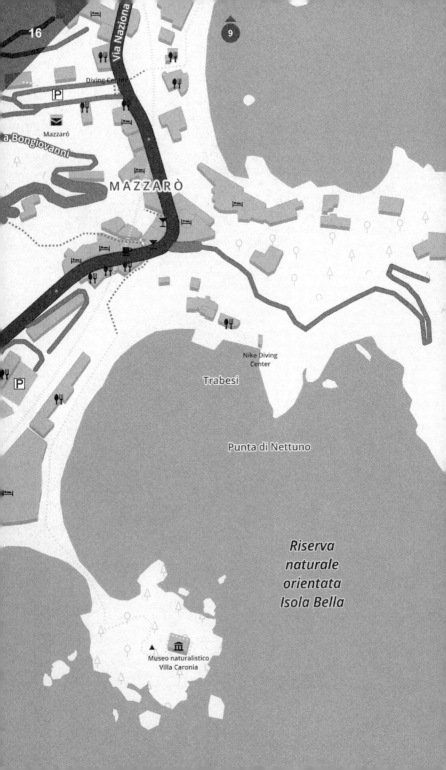

9

Via Naziona

Diving Center

P

✉ Mazzaró

a Bongiovanni

MAZZARÒ

P

Nike Diving
Center

Trabesi

Punta di Nettuno

*Riserva
naturale
orientata
Isola Bella*

🏛

Museo naturalistico
Villa Caronia

Grotta di
Sant'Andrea

Sifone Capo Sant'Andrea
- scuba

Gorgonie
Capo Sant'Andrea

Grotta Azzurra

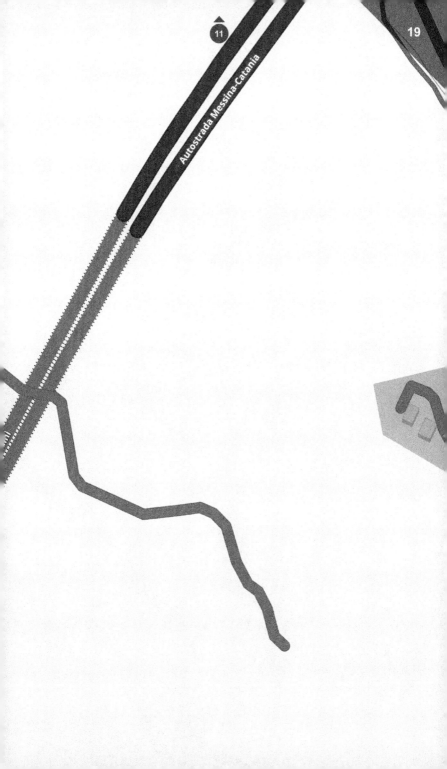

Autostrada Messina-Catania

Via Madonna delle Grazie

Taormina-
Giardini

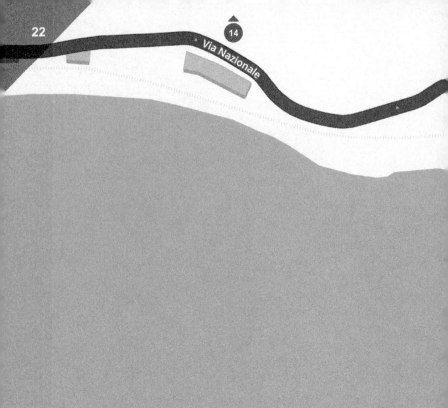

P

P

Grotta la
Conchiglia

Lido Conchiglie

Lido Conchiglie

Grotta Bunker

Grotta la
Bolla (scuba)

I Faragl

Colonne romane
(scuba)

Gorgonie Capo Taorr
(scuba)

Streets

A

Autostrada messina-
    catania 3, 7, 8, 11, 12,
    18, 19

C

Contrada mastrissa . . 10,
    11, 18–20
Contrada ortogrande 19,
    20
Corso umberto i . . 12–14,
    20

F

Fosso martelletto . . . 4, 5

G

Galleria capopietre 3
Galleria giardini . . . 18, 19
Galleria isolabella 15
Galleria sant'antonio 3, 8
Galleria spisone 8
Galleria svincolo 3
Galleria taormina 6, 7, 12,
    13

L

Largo degli eponomi . 12
Largo san giorgio 5
Lungomare regina
    margherita 20

P

Piazza 9 aprile 13
Piazza andromaco 12

Piazza cacciola 6
Piazza carmine 13
Piazza del duomo 13
Piazza del tocco 12
Piazza della garitella . . 5
Piazza duomo 5
Piazza johann wolfgang
    goethe 12
Piazza paladini 13
Piazza ragia 14
Piazza san domenico
    de guzman 13
Piazza san francesco di
    paola 12
Piazza san giorgio 5
Piazza sant'antonino . . 5
Piazza sant'antonio
    abate 12
Piazza santa caterina . 14
Piazza santa domenica
    14
Piazza varo 13
Piazza vittorio
    emanuele ii 14
Piazzetta calapitrulli . . 14
Piazzetta salvatore
    leone 13

S

Salita acropoli 13
Salita appia 13
Salita badia vecchia . . 13
Salita dei gracchi 13
Salita della scalazza . . . 4
Salita delle ginestre . . 6
Salita di castelmola . . 12,
    13
Salita franceso de luna
    13
Salita giuseppe capri . 13
Salita guglielmo melvia
    13

Salita ibrahim 12, 13
Salita lucio denti 13
Salita palazzo ciampoli
    13
Salita santippo 13, 14
Scesa bastione 13
Scesa morgana 13
Sentiero dei saraceni . 4,
    5, 12
Stairs to taormina 15

T

Traversa alcide de
    gasperi 5
Traversa contrada
    nazionale 8
Traversa via tutti i santi 5

V

Via agrigento 20
Via alcide de gasperi . 4,
    5
Via annunziata 4, 5
Via apollo arcageta . . 12
Via bagnoli croce . 14, 15
Via bastione 13
Via bonfacio 13
Via bongiovanni . . 15, 16
Via branco . . . 5, 6, 12, 13
Via cajo numitorio 14
Via calabrò 5
Via calapitrulli 13, 14
Via calvario 12
Via calzolai 5
Via cannone 5
Via cariddi 20
Via case pinte 13
Via castellucio 9
Via catania 20
Via censimento 20

Via cesare ottaviano . . 12
Via cinquefonti 20
Via circonvallazione . 13,
14
Via circonvallazione sud
4, 5
Via conte ruggero 13
Via corrado cagli 12
Via costantino patricio 5,
14
Via crocifisso 12, 20
Via crucis 13
Via cuculunazzo 5
Via cuseni 12
Via cutrufelli 7, 14
Via damiano russo . . . 13
Via degli strategi 14
Via dei fabi 13
Via dei naxi 14
Via dei saraceni 12
Via dei sei molini 20
Via del ghetto 12
Via della chiusa 12
Via delle trombe 5
Via dietro cappuccini . 6,
13, 14
Via dietro la noce 14
Via dionisio i 12, 13
Via domenico di leo . . 12
Via don giovanni bosco
13, 14
Via don giovanni min-
zoni 14
Via ficarella 5
Via fontana vecchia . . . 6,
13, 14
Via fontanelle . 11, 19, 20
Via fortuna 5
Via francesco strazzeri
14
Via fratelli bandiera . . 13,
14
Via fratelli ingegnere . 14
Via giardinazzo 13, 14
Via ginnasio 14
Via giovanni di giovanni
14
Via girolamo savonarola
13
Via giuseppe verdi 13, 14
Via guardiola vecchia 14,
15
Via guglielmo marconi
14, 15
Via iallia bassia 14
Via ii gisofat 5
Via iv gisofat 5

Via le mura 14
Via leonardo da vinci . 4,
5, 12, 13
Via leto 5
Via luigi pirandello . . . 14,
15, 22, 23
Via madonna delle gra-
zie 13, 14,
21
Via madonna rocca . . 13
Via marconi 20
Via mario e nicolò
garipoli 7, 8
Via medaglia d'oro 5
Via messina 20
Via michele amari 13
Via molino 20
Via montello 20
Via mulino 20
Via naumachie 13, 14
Via nazionale . 3, 8, 9, 15,
16, 20-23
Via ortogrande 20
Via ospedale 12
Via otto geleng 12
Via paladini 13
Via paternò di biscari . 12
Via piano porto 8
Via pietro rizzo 12, 13
Via pio ix 5
Via pitagora 13
Via porta di mola 5
Via porta pasquale . . 7, 8
Via rabbia 5
Via ragia 14
Via robert kitson . . . 11, 12
Via roma . . . 13, 14, 20, 21
Via s. gullotta 5
Via salita castello 5
Via san domenico 13
Via san giorgio 5
Via san leo 14
Via san nicola 20
Via san nicolò 5
Via san pietro 15
Via sant'antonino 5
Via santa maria dei
greci 13
Via sesto pompeo 12
Via sibilla 4, 5
Via siracusa 20
Via sirina 20
Via slipigni 7, 14
Via sottoporta 5
Via spisone 8
Via strabone 13
Via stretta 5

Via teatrino romano . . 14
Via teatro greco 14
Via timeo 13, 14
Via timoleone 14
Via tommaso fazzello 12,
13
Via tribuna 5
Via trieste 20
Via tutti i santi 5
Via vallone castagna . . 8
Via vecchio macello . . 14
Via verdi 5
Via vincenzo bellini . . . 5
Via wilhelm von glöden
12
Viadotto sirina . 11, 12, 19
Viale italia 14
Viale pietro toselli 12
Viale san pancrazio . . 14
Vico ascanio marziani 13
Vico cieco del ginnasio
14
Vico claudio marcello 14
Vico cleone 13, 14
Vico de spuches . . 12, 13
Vico degli ebrei 13
Vico dei siculi 12
Vico dei vespri siciliani
14
Vico del ginnasio 14
Vico ennio sirio 14
Vico giovanni crupi . . . 13
Vico gregorio cerameo
14
Vico interdonato 12
Vico la floresta 13
Vico lombardo 13
Vico pirro 14
Vico polibio 12
Vico romano 13
Vico sacramento 13
Vico san francesco di
paola 12
Vico san pancrazio . . . 14
Vico santa domenica . 14
Vico saraceni 5
Vico sibilla 4, 5
Vico teocle 13
Vico teofane ceromeo
13
Vico tindarione 14
Vico venezia 13
Vico zecca 14
Vicolo san nicolò 5
Vicolo stretto 13

Points of Interest

A

Ancient Greek Theater
👤 14
Archeological Museum
🏛 13

B

Bay Isola Bella 👤 . . . 16
Bus Station (Piazza
L.Piradello-Via
L.Piradello 36) 🚌
14

C

Canyon del Diablo-
Scuba Point 👤 . . . 16
Carabinieri Police HQ 🚔
14
Castello Castelmola 👤 5
Castello on Monte
Tauro 👤 13
Cathedral San Nicoló di
Bari 👤 13
Church and View Point
San Biagio 👤 4
Church San Antonio
Abate (P.Toseli 2) 👤
12
Church San Giorgio 👤 . 5
Church San Giuseppe
(Piazza 9 Aprile) 👤
13
Church San Michele
Ancangelo (P.Rizzo
12) 👤 13
Church San Nicoló di
Bari 👤 5
Church San Pancazio
(Viale San Pan-
cazio) 👤 14

Church Santa Caterina
👤 14
Church Santissima An-
nunziata 👤 4
Clock Tower and View
Point in Piazza 9
Aprile 👤 13
Commune di Taormina-
Town Hall 👤 13
Culture Venue-Former
Church Carmine 🏛
13

G

Grotta Azzura 👤 17
Grotta Bunker 👤 23
Grotta dei Camberi 👤 23
Grotta di Spisone-Cave
👤 8
Grotta e Piscinette Nat-
urali Sant'Andrea 👤
17
Grotta la Bolla 👤 23
Grotta la Conchiglia 👤
23

H

Hospital San Vincenzo
✚ 20

M

Mazzaro 🏢 16
Mazzaro-Taormina Ca-
ble Car Lower Sta-
tion (Via Nationale
232) 🚠 16
Mazzaro-Taormina Ca-
ble Car Top Station

(L.Pirandello 22) 🚠
14
Mercato-Municipal Mar-
ket 👤 14
Museum of Nature Villa
Caronia 🏛 16
Museum of Popular
Traditions (Vico
San Francesco di
Paola-Right to Via
O.Geleng) 🏛 12

N

Necropolis of Cocolon-
azzo 👤 5

O

Old Roman Wells of
Ancient Milia 👤 . . . 5
Open Air Museum-Rock
Village 🏛 9

P

Palazzo Ciampoli (Salita
Palazzo Right to
Corso Umberto I)
👤 13
Palazzo Corvaja (Piazza
V.Emanuelle II) 🏛 14
Palazzo Duchi di Santo
Stefano 👤 12
Piazza and View Point
San Antonio 👤 . . . 5
Porta Catania (Corso
Umberto I) 👤 12
Porta Messina (Corso
Umberto I) 👤 14
Public Swimming Pool
🏃 15

Printed in Great Britain
by Amazon